MONEY GROWS ON TREES

Title: Money Grows On Trees

Author: Kambiz Mostofizadeh

Publisher: Mikazuki Publishing House

ISBN-13: 978-1-942825-44-9

Description: Money Grows on Trees teaches you the secrets of making money using passive income.

MONEY GROWS ON TREES

Introduction

If you read 25 Principles of Strategy, Grow Rich, and Secrets of Making Money, then you will have an understanding of the business principles and their applications as I have previously explained them. Money Grows On Trees expands on the business ideas and methods that I have explained in the 25 Principles of Strategy, Grow Rich, and Secrets of Making Money. If you are motivated and you are seeking to make passive income, then Money Grows On Trees will provide you with a concrete roadmap for achieving that success. In business, as in life, there are no guarantees that anyone will achieve success. But it is guaranteed that if you do nothing, then you will achieve nothing.

MONEY GROWS ON TREES

MGOT System

The MGOT system depends on you
being able to create 7 streams of
Passive Income. In Grow Rich, I
referred to this as Active Revenue
Channels (ARC). Active Revenue
Channels create synergy and allow you
to generate income at a faster pace.
You do not have to be rich to create
passive income. You need to be
motivated and you have to be
dedicated, but you do not have to be
rich. You have to be willing to take the
steps to achieve success and that
depends on you putting in the time and
effort required to see results. There are
various things that can generate passive
income for you on a monthly basis but
there are ways that can be generated
that are better than others. What makes
one passive income ARC more valuable

MONEY GROWS ON TREES

than another one? Productivity. What is your output in dollars for the amount of time invested? Some passive income revenue streams are not worth their time. As an example, I have over 400 music songs on various music streaming networks. I do generate passive income from these 400 songs, but was the time I invested in making these 400 songs worth it? No. I spent 26 years of my life making music and performing on stages, but the amount of money I generated was not worth the time I invested. My songs still do generate money on a monthly basis but the amount is so low (and embarrassing) that it is not worth mentioning. I was just providing you with an example of a passive income revenue stream that has not been worth the time I invested in it. If I have 4000 songs, will I make more money? Yes, but the time I will have to invest to make 4000 songs could have spent on another passive income revenue stream that was more lucrative. Some of your revenue streams will be able to generate more for you than other revenue streams and that is a natural effect in business.

Failure Is Not An Option

Everyone is so scared of failing that they never start anything so that they will never fail. Their reasoning is flawed because if you never start anything then it is not possible for you to fail. You have to do something in order to win or fail at it. If you never do anything out of fear of failure then it is not possible for you to fail or win in that situation. Why are people so scared of failure? Do they

MONEY GROWS ON TREES

think that others will judge them and ridicule them? Let us say that you start 10 businesses and 9 of them fail, should you be judged for the 9 businesses that failed or should you be judged for the 1 business that was a success? Depends on who you are asking. Some people will say the person is a failure in life because they failed at 9 businesses despite 1 eventually becoming a success. What if you were told that chocolate titan of industry Milton Hershey went bankrupt multiple times before he became a success? What if you found that the greatest entrepreneurial minds to have ever lived failed multiple times before becoming successful? What is the worst that is going to happen to you if you fail in a business? You can start a new business with the added bonus of having first

MONEY GROWS ON TREES

hand experience of what your previous business fail. You gained experience that cost you time and money and you are now able to take that experience with you in to your other ventures. It is a mistake for someone that became successful in finance or in real estate to think that they are an all knowing entrepreneur. Struggling and becoming a success is not the same as failing in multiple businesses. Failing in multiple businesses means you have personally started more than 10 businesses that have failed. As the business saying goes, Fail Fast. If you are to fail, it is better to fail fast and take those experiences with you unto your other business ventures. You paid for that experience and that experience can only be gotten by loss (which you have experienced). Just as in life you should

MONEY GROWS ON TREES

not sit and dwell on past failures (other than to learn from them), so too in business you should not look back at past business failures other than to learn from and apply those lessons to new business ventures you will be attempting in the future. A person that has never failed cannot be trusted to run anything at all. A business master is a businessperson that has made every mistake possible. Success has never bred more success just based on luck. It is to the contrary. So many businesspersons that achieved success through luck on their first attempt had massive losses and failures to show in the future. That is because their first success was lucky and could not be re-created on other business ventures. A business master does not work based on luck. A business master works based

MONEY GROWS ON TREES

on knowing the many mistakes that could occur if certain steps are not taken. A business person that has never erred is more likely than not a novice. Even billionaire Warren Buffett has made mistakes. Everyone has made mistakes in business and everyone has had a business fail. Be wary of a business person that claims that they have been successful their whole life. Everyone has taken losses, big or small. Everyone has seen their business venture sour or take a loss. It is a natural part of business and anyone that says otherwise has never done business and has never created jobs. There are some self proclaimed business critics that think that every business should be a success for every person on earth. It just doesn't work that way. There are many reasons why a

MONEY GROWS ON TREES

person can fail at business and it can be various factors affecting the health of that business. Each instance has to be examined in detail to understand the factors involved as well as the conditions that led to the failure of that business. There are some start up companies that started with hundreds of millions of dollars and failed. There are start up companies that started with billions of dollars and failed. There are start up companies that started with $30,000 and grew to $500,000,000. The first rule of money is never lose control of your money. No one can make a decision for you better than you can. If you hand your money over to someone else, they will decide for you. It is your money and it is your right to decide what you want to do with it. If you decide to spend it on an investment then

MONEY GROWS ON TREES

that is your choice. It is up to you to make informed decisions. The first decision you must make is never lose control of your money. Once you lose control of your money, it is expensive and difficult to get it back. It takes a long time to recover from financial loss. It takes a long time to bounce back after setbacks or defeat. You will only prolong the length of your recovery by trusting your money to others. Make your own informed investment decisions and you will see the benefits of your actions. Negative people have a way of bringing others down to their level. They want others to also feel negative and depressed just because they are negative and depressed. What they need is motivation and they need the will to win. You can't be micro-managed on the way to success. If you become

MONEY GROWS ON TREES

successful you can only thank yourself
and if you fail you can only blame
yourself. If you want to succeed you
have to learn to remove negative and
toxic people from your life. You should
not have your ambitions crushed
because someone else is un-easy with
your drive for success. If you want to
become a success, you have to avoid
negative and toxic people, simply
because their negativity and toxicity is
contagious. They have the mindset that
nothing should be tried because you
could fail. Because they have never
done anything they fear that you will
actually do something and become
successful at it. They want you to do
nothing so that they can have the
satisfaction they are right and you are
wrong. Anything you propose to them is
wrong because they have a negative

MONEY GROWS ON TREES

and toxic attitude towards growth. They want to play it safe and playing it safe means doing absolutely nothing will the clock keeps ticking away. How many ticks do you think you have before your clock stops ticking? No one can tell you that with certainty, but the one certainty that we all do face is that of time. Time is finite and fleeting. Time is not on your side unless you are invested in progress. Doing nothing does not make the rest of the world stop doing something. Doing nothing is actually more dangerous and risky than doing something. Do you think the prices of real estate or gold or other assets stop rising just because you have decided to do nothing and to wait and see what happens. I will tell you what happens. Time just keeps going and the prices of everything on earth keep rising. That is

MONEY GROWS ON TREES

what happens. It is called inflation and it is a reality anywhere on earth. As new money is generated by everyone on earth, you are sitting and doing nothing. The price of real estate and gold and other assets keep rising to beat inflation and that means life gets more expensive for you every year. Over the past 100 years, real estate prices have safely and steadily risen. Everything keeps rising in price as the value of your money decreases. A 5 bedroom house in Los Angeles had a price tag of $300,000 in 2000. What is the price of that home today? $1,500,000. That is a 5 times (500%) increase in 20 years. A 2 bedroom apartment in Las Vegas had a price tag of $50,000 in 2015. What is the price of that home today? $150,000. That is a 3 times increase (300%) in 5 years. Do you have more buying power

MONEY GROWS ON TREES

today in comparison to 5 years ago? No.
The price of food, gasoline, as well as
utilities have increased. The overall cost
of living has increased in major and
minor cities. As the price of real estate
and gold increase, retail shops and
wholesalers raise their prices to not fall
behind. Soon, everyone is raising prices
on everything so they do not fall behind.
This causes the prices of everything to
rise and to lower your quality of life.
Doing nothing will not make you rich and
there are many signs that it could make
you poor in the future. If you do nothing,
then you have gained nothing, but you
doing nothing has absolutely no effect
on the prices of real estate and gold
rising. They will continue rising whether
you do something or if you do nothing.
This is why it is so important to move
your money in to investments that can at

MONEY GROWS ON TREES

least beat the rate of inflation. If you don't, then your money will be of less value next year in comparison to this year. This is an un-changeable reality that has to be understood and accordingly adjusted to. You have to keep finding new vehicles (real estate or business or gold) that will provide you with a rate of return that is higher than that of the rate of inflation. Inflation is most certainly caused by an increase in the money supply. If everyone on earth is investing or working and generating new money, do you think the increase in money supply will raise or lower the value of your money? It will most certainly lower the value of your money which is why your money is not worth the same amount next year. While you are doing nothing to stay completely safe from loss, the value of your money

MONEY GROWS ON TREES

lowers and this also has an effect on the rise of real estate prices (and other assets as well). Business cannot be avoided for the sake of safety. Business has to be embraced for the sake of future security. If the business successful, it will open many new doors for you in other investment avenues. If it fails, then it was a learning experience for you. Let us say that you try something new in business and you do fail. Did the world end? Did you die? Is your reputation tarnished? No. You learned from it and gained real world business experience. Business experience is either learned from others or it is learned firsthand. It costs money to gain that knowledge regarding the vast world of business. You can acquire that knowledge from fortune-tellers and you cannot acquire that knowledge by

MONEY GROWS ON TREES

thinking about it. Business experience costs money and time. Business experience took effort to be gained. If you don't do business, how will you learn it? In any given business investment, a myriad of problems could arise. Do you quit at the first sign of trouble? If you do, then you may not be a good business investor. A business investor has to be willing to weather the storm and accept the current difficulties and move past them in order to get to the future rewards. It is difficult to bear complex situations that last for periods of time. You have to be thick-skinned in business and be able to take two steps back in order to take one step forward. Every angel investor or venture capitalist has faced difficult, hardship, and setbacks from their various business investments. If it were easy,

MONEY GROWS ON TREES

then everyone would be rich. You will read article after article arguing for luck and against the belief that luck has anything to do with business. Does luck exist and if it does exist, what role does it play in my business? You can call it what you wish, but it is indeed a reality that some individuals have access to more resources than you do. They have access to more contacts than you do. Luck has been explained away as being a consequence of deliberate steps to prepare beforehand for the future. Preparation is indeed a vital factor in your success but is preparation alone sufficient to explain why a business fails and why it thrives? Luck can be explained as the right pieces working in synchronicity to deliver the desired result. But this would still not be sufficient to explain luck for the

MONEY GROWS ON TREES

aforementioned explanation would still be tied to preparation. Luck gives you success when the odds are stacked against you. When your chances of winning are low and you still win, that is a clear sign of luck. Your business is affected by luck and no amount of preparation beforehand can guarantee success. Even if you have thoroughly and meticulously prepared beforehand, your chances of winning are still low enough to determine a loss rather than a victory. Therefore it is luck that gives you victory. Can you make your own luck? No. Being in the right place at the right time will create luck. You can underestimate luck as much as you wish but it has played a crucial role in the creation of millionaires and billionaires. They will all tell you that they achieved it by their hard work and hard work is

MONEY GROWS ON TREES

surely a factor in their success. They will omit telling you the most important reason for their success which is luck. People get lucky all the time, just ask a Lottery winner that won 200 million dollars. That person randomly chose some numbers and got lucky when their numbers were called. Was that Lottery winner a psychic or did that Lottery winner have someone giving them the winning numbers? No. That person got lucky and that is all that happened. They got lucky and won. There is no formula for winning a Lottery, There is no secret method for picking Lottery numbers. The person just got lucky and won. People get lucky all the time and the lottery winner is a perfect example of a person that has benefitted in real life from luck. If you put yourself in the right place at the right time, you too could get lucky.

MONEY GROWS ON TREES

We were all born poor but none of us are forced to die poor. You change your future by being pro-active and chasing business. You change your future by being pro-active and making sales on a daily basis. It is up to you to change your financial well being. No one is responsible for your financial well being. You are responsible for your financial well being. If you become poor, your friends may even celebrate your downfall. If you become poor, people that you thought will support will turn their back on you. Everyone wants to be friends with someone who is rich. No one wants to become friends with someone who is poor or that asks you for money. You have to take charge of your financial well being by actively seeking new business opportunities and by seeking new customers to sell to. If

MONEY GROWS ON TREES

you are able to have consistency and patience, then you will eventually reach your goals. You will not win anything in business by having a negative attitude. You will not win anything in business by blaming the world for your lack of success. You have to make the decision that you are going to change your financial status by seeking business opportunities. You have to make the decision that you are going to change your financial status by seeking new customers. No one can do it for you. You are the Captain of your Financial Future. Opportunities are time based. If an opportunity is not seized at the time that it presents itself, then the opportunity will pass. This is an important understanding that you must accept in business. Opportunities pass by and the person that seizes on the

MONEY GROWS ON TREES

opportunity receives the benefits from the risk. Every opportunity is, in one form or another, a risk. A risk for winning and a risk for losing. Without the correct timing, an opportunity will not appear nor can an opportunity be exploited. Business depends on timing. All of the pieces have to be together for the opportunity to exist. For those that create their own opportunity, they are benefitting from arranging the time to win. If you are able to put together the pieces to create opportunity then you are also creating the timing for you to win. In most conditions, the pieces have to exist and fall in to place themselves. You cannot bypass conditions, for if the proper conditions are not met to create an opportunity, all one can do is wait for it. Opportunists understanding timing and conditions, which is why they are

MONEY GROWS ON TREES

able to quickly identify when an opportunity presents itself. You cannot force the creation of opportunities. Opportunities can force the creation of Windows Of Opportunity (WOO). By taking advantage of a WOO by investing in it, you are able to reap the benefits of doing so. Imagine if you had bought Amazon stock in 1997. Your investment would have increased many times over the past twenty some years. You would have benefitted by taking advantage of a WOO. On a daily basis, we are presented with opportunities of every kind imaginable. Whether we seize on those opportunities is our choice. In most cases, we choose to do nothing, because doing nothing sometimes feels like the best thing to do. Getty or Hershey didn't build business empires by waiting or by doing nothing. They

MONEY GROWS ON TREES

were always doing something. Inactivity is equal to being non-operational or non-functional. As long as you are moving upwards and forward towards your success, you are winning. A loser is a person that gives up in the face of difficulty. A loser is a person that searches for excuses and for reasons why something will not work. Everyone is clever to an extent and many want to prove how clever they are by attempting to disprove your ideas. Every business idea is an opportunity that can be developed with an org chart, business model, and funding, in to a viable business. Some businesses started with hundreds of millions of dollars and went bankrupt. Some businesses started with nearly nothing and became hugely successful. No one has a crystal ball with the ability to foresee future

MONEY GROWS ON TREES

business events. If fortune tellers were real, then they would be able to predict and change their own futures, would they not? All business is speculation and speculative action. A WOO is a way to profit (or take a loss) by speculating. Money has a value that is dynamic. Money raises or drops in value based on several factors and the Purchasing Power Parity is an effect of that. A WOO allows you speculate by investing in an idea, start-up, or property in order to reap the benefits of its appreciation. Land appreciates and rises in value. Gold, has historically, risen and appreciated in value. Since money has a future value, an investor seeks to hedge themselves against inflation by putting their money in a financial vehicle that will provide them the highest value. Each financial vehicle has an average

MONEY GROWS ON TREES

rate of return on your investment. It is important to try to find the investment vehicles with the higher rate of investment. Some would argue that real estate is the best financial vehicle. Some would argue that Gold is the greatest financial vehicle. It is up to you to do as much research as possible to understand the strengths and weaknesses of the various financial vehicles. Time is your friend and you have to make use of time by not wasting it on frivolous activities. You have to focus on achieving success, no matter how many setbacks you experience in your personal and business life. Success is not handed to you rather that success is earned through hard work and focused efforts. Anyone that received anything on a silver platter, ended up not being able to make money

MONEY GROWS ON TREES

so they had to sell the silver platter. Once you are an experienced and savvy business and real estate investor, you will be the one holding all the silver platters. You will be able to buy gifts for your friends and family, you will be able to buy the home you always wanted, you will not be ashamed of having things that you deserve, and you will be a happier and more productive member of society. Money changes lives and it can and will change your life permanently. You have to be pro-active and bring in the money as the money will not chase you. You have to chase your dreams and money is an effect of your activities. No one can be you and that is your super-human power in life. You have to choose success and choose to be around others that are involved in chasing success or have

MONEY GROWS ON TREES

found success. You have to believe in yourself when no one else does. You have to believe in what you want to accomplish. You have to believe that you can be successful and you have to believe that you deserve success. There are thousands of ways to get rich and they include investing in businesses, investing in gold, investing in stocks, and investing in real estate. The vast majority of millionaires became rich through real estate. Real estate is not easy to get rich off. There is nothing that is easy in life or in anything. Anything that is achieved is done so by hard work and long hours of dedication. Get rich schemes are more likely than not Ponzi schemes or pyramid schemes. Real Estate is not digital coin you can't touch or feel. You can touch real estate and you can repair and upgrade real estate.

MONEY GROWS ON TREES

Real estate will increase in value over time while you are sleeping. Real Estate will, over 100 years, increase in value and it will make you rich over 30 years. You will not get rich overnight but you will get rich over 30 years. The sooner you start on your journey the sooner you will be on the road to riches but you will not get anywhere by brooding in a pool of pity and doing nothing. Everyone has had setbacks, delays, losses, and heartbreaks. You have to use your setbacks as fuel for your internal drive. You have to take your will and drive to succeed and apply it to the real world. You cannot be afraid of being successful. Buying real estate using owner financing is nothing new and it has been done by tens of thousands of people in the past 10 years. Buying timber land is nothing new as has been

MONEY GROWS ON TREES

done by tens of thousands of people in the past. It is the knowledge of what to do with the drive to make it happen that makes what you are learning worth it. You have to be willing to go and see properties from up close and to judge them in a standard way. You have to understand what the signs are that makes a property valuable rather than a money pit. You have to have good taste and good judgment and the ability to choose between hundreds of properties you find. You have to a Success driven mindset that powers you forward in the face of uncertainty and various issues that need to be resolved. You will earn in life what you work for and you have to work smart and frugal. No one has to believe in what you are doing as long as you believe that you are going to be successful. You have to have the

MONEY GROWS ON TREES

mindset that you are holding a flashlight in the dark and you are leading the path to success. You are trailblazing and creating your own path to success by taking the necessary to achieve it. Naysayers, negative, and toxic people should be avoided at all costs. Since they do not want to take the necessary steps to achieve success they attempt to convince others that they can never have it. No one is the master of your destiny but you. Once you make the conscious decision to become successful and to become rich, your mind has a way of adjusting your perception and reality to achieve it. Your mind is the most powerful weapon you have and it can make you become successful. Not by thinking about it, but by doing it. By putting in the hours needed to find the right properties to

MONEY GROWS ON TREES

buy, doing your due diligence in order to make sure there are no pitfalls or negatives attached to the sale, placing multiple offers on multiple properties, correctly doing the legal paperwork with the help of a Real Estate Lawyer, fixing up the property (cosmetic and structural), renting out the property to a qualified renter, and re-financing the property. It is easier said than done but so are many things worth achieving in life. They take time and effort in order to be achieved. Get rich fast schemes don't work but get rich slow schemes do work and have proven themselves to work. If you are willing to put in the time, you will see the results. Everyone gets jealous when viewing someone else get rich without acknowledging the difficult and time involved to get rich. It is easy to judge others but difficult to be honest

MONEY GROWS ON TREES

with ourselves. If you want to get rich, then you have to take the steps to get you rich. You have to put in the time to make you rich. If you want a salary, then get a job. If you want to get rich through real estate, then you have to be willing to be energetic and focused on achieving the success you have envisioned. You deserve the best in life. You deserve to own a home and own a car and own a boat. It takes effort on your part to realize it and it takes time to bring it to fruition. If you use your time wisely and manage your time, you can find properties and visit them. You can analyze and compare properties and make offers on them. You can find lenders that will re-finance them. All investments are speculation. Nobody can tell you with one hundred percent certainty that a financial vehicle or an

MONEY GROWS ON TREES

investment, will make you a profit. We invest with the hope that we can make a profit. All investments are educated guesses at best and are gambling at worst. On a gambling table, you place your money on something, for example red or black at a roulette table. There is no guarantee of winning but there is a good chance that you will in fact lose your money. Investing in real estate, is not a guarantee, that you will win. It is a speculation. Like all speculations, you are optimistic and have hope that you will succeed by profiting. In most scenarios, it is difficult to lose by investing in real estate. You will be surprised by the amount of millionaires and billionaires that have gone heavily in debt or became bankrupt through real estate speculation. Speculation is a form of gambling. You wish for the ideal

MONEY GROWS ON TREES

situation to materialize. If it does you will brag about it to everyone. If you lose, you will start to hate the game and will want to stop playing all together. The game is not flawed. Your decisions can, however, be heavily flawed. The best real estate investors have an accountant that tells them whether it makes to invest in a certain property. An accountant consulting you is far better than a real estate agent consulting you on profits and losses. The real estate agent can present you with properties but your accountant will have to tell you if you will profit or lose by investing your money in it. Real estate investments are speculative like gambling, except that real estate has proven itself over the past 100 years, as a relatively safe investment vehicle for slow and steady growth. Real estate investors

MONEY GROWS ON TREES

understand this and seek to take advantage of this "blue chip" safe investment for reaching their goals. Real estate always rises though there are several times in history when real estate has dropped in value. Although there definitely have been times when it dropped in value, real estate has risen steadily in value over the past 100 years. The times when real estate did drop in the United States, are much less than the times that the price of real estate rose. Real estate, can be viewed as the safest and surest way to grow rich over 30 years. If there are people that have gone bankrupt because of real estate, it is because they purchased real estate in a worthless location, they did not have enough of their own capital invested and depended too heavily on loans, and/or were not able to monetize

MONEY GROWS ON TREES

their property. Real estate is the safest form of investment but it is important to have enough capital invested in order to minimize the amount of loan needed (if any). The ideal situation is to purchase a property outright and to not have any open liability. There are several places where property can be purchased for under $100,000. If you are able to spend a large amount of time in research to gain an understanding of real estate prices and the opportunities available, then you will be able to purchase property faster and with greater ease. Even if you do not have the money for a down payment, you can negotiate with an Owner Financed property to absorb the Down Payment in to the Monthly Payments for that buying that property. There are several ways you can do this but it is important to

MONEY GROWS ON TREES

have the mindset of being open to using Creative Financing when purchasing property. Many property owners prefer to not deal with banks or mortgage companies and to transact directly with the buyer of the property. By using creative financing, the range of properties available to you increases.

Yes you do deserve success. Not everyone will be successful because not everyone is willing to put in the effort it takes to become successful. Your mindset has to be focused around your success without you becoming sidetracked on new adventures that will take up your time. Do one thing and do that one thing very well. A master of all trades is a master of none. You have to keep doing it until you are both confident in your abilities as well as being familiar

MONEY GROWS ON TREES

with the owner financing sales process. Avoid toxic people that say you can't do it. What they are really telling you is that they can't do it. You can do anything you want as long as you put your mind to it. You can achieve any level of success that you can dream of as long as you are willing to work for it. You have to be strong on the inside as well as on the outside. You have to be thick skinned and focused on completing property deals. There are no shortcuts and no easy routes to success. As long as the steps are followed, everyone can be successful using this system. Owner financing real estate is not new and has been done so many times that it is routine (and mundane). The real estate is not going to jump in to your lap. You have to find it and that means searching anywhere and everywhere you can. You

MONEY GROWS ON TREES

have to be pro-active in order to generate passive income. Let us say that together. You have to be pro-active in order to generate passive income. You have to hunt for the deals so that you have a pool of choices to choose from. The more choices you have the better the property you will find. It all comes down to choice and choosing the wrong property can make you liable to various costs that you would not incur had you searched for a wide range of properties. The more choices, the better the choice. Owner financed properties are not always pretty. You are going to search through many properties before you arrive at a few good ones. There are a lot of properties that are not worth investing in because they have serious structural damages that could require tens of thousands of dollars of work.

MONEY GROWS ON TREES

You have to spend the time searching in order to find a wide range of properties that you could entertain investing in. Some of them required minimal cosmetic repairs and some of them require structural repairs. Construction costs rack up fast and are costly. You cannot expect to find a pretty home for a low cost. You are more likely to find a large number of ugly homes that have expenses ranging from past due payments to construction. Owner financed homes must be re-habilitated and re-modeled for maintenance purposes and so that you are able to rent out that property to a renter for a higher price. Spending actual time finding owner financed homes and going through the sales process for the first time will teach you through experience. After your first success, you will feel like

MONEY GROWS ON TREES

you are flying on the clouds. Could this really be possible? Yes. If you were un- aware of owner financed deals then you are not alone. There are hundreds of millions of people that are not aware that they can purchase a home using owner financing. The reason they don't do it is because they have no experience in doing it, so they avoid it all together. If you do nothing at all then you have no risk whatsoever. In other words, if you take no risks you are completely safe financially but then you will gain nothing. Nothing ventured, nothing gained was as true as when it was said. You have to be willing to take risks in order to win. Every investment vehicle is a form of speculation. You have no way of 100 percent being guaranteed anything. But if you take the steps that people have taken before

MONEY GROWS ON TREES

successfully, then you will stand to gain from their knowledge and experience. What one person can do another can do, is a true statement. Buying owner financed properties are a standard way of purchasing property for individuals that have bad credit, are over-extended in their credit, are out of work, or have no credit. It is a way for buyers to lift themselves out of poverty by owning something that is both valuable and real. Real Estate can be lived in, used as an office, used as collateral for loans, and can be developed (townhouses, condominiums, apartments, houses, stores, etc.). It has real value which is why Banks own it. There are many people that have lost money in real estate as well, but the reason is less benign than you imagine. People that lost money in real estate made bad

MONEY GROWS ON TREES

business decisions that cost them money and years of their life. You never invest more than you can and you never become over-extended. To do so would put your entire portfolio at risk. Spending hundreds of millions or losing hundreds of millions of dollars is a game for the ultra-rich one percent. In reality, most real estate is obtainable through owner financing if the down payment and loan terms satisfy the seller. It is up to the buyer to be creative in financing and to find ways to satisfy a seller. If the Seller asks for $20,000 down on a $200,000 house, you can ask for the seller to amortize the down payment in to monthly payments that are manageable. If you had to, you could even make an offer on a home that is higher than other bids, if you are able to amortize the down payment in to monthly payments.

MONEY GROWS ON TREES

Some sellers may appreciate that for various reasons. A homeowner facing pre-foreclosure just might appreciate the offer to buy their home while paying off their delinquent payments. Each seller has their own unique reason for selling and it is frankly none of the buyer's business, why they are selling it. The seller may have a myriad of reasons for selling it but as long as they are willing to entertain selling it to you on an owner financed basis, they are then an option that you could use when buying. In the beginning of your journey, start off with lower priced homes, under $50,000. As you gain experience buying owner financed homes you can raise your limit to under $100,000. It is important to keep repeating the process in order to be successful and to Grow Rich. Repetition causes familiarity and allows you to become comfortable enough with the process that you are confident in your abilities. The more confident you become, the larger the deals you will seek to transact. It is important to start from the ground level and work your way up in order to acquire a firm grasp on the fundamentals of purchasing owner financed homes.

The Process

Find Properties – You should spend most of your time sifting through various websites, newspapers, and media outlets in order to find potential properties for bidding on.

Due Diligence – Visit the property and check for damages (cosmetic and structural) or issues that should be

MONEY GROWS ON TREES

addressed. Have Real Estate Lawyer read your Offer before you make it.

Make an Offer – Offer to buy the property using the "Subject to" clause in the contract.

Sign Contract – Use a Real Estate Lawyer and an Official Notary.

Deed & Title – Have Real Estate put in your name.

Rehab – Fix up the property in order to prepare it to be rented.

Rent – Rent out the property using comparable properties nearby to establish a fair value for rental prices or use a real estate agent to determine the monthly rental price of your newly acquired real estate.

MONEY GROWS ON TREES

The formula is simple. Buy in to passive income or create new streams of passive income. The easiest way to buy in to passive income is to become an investor. You don't need an MBA from a fancy university to become an investor. You don't need a license or a degree to invest in real estate. You need money, courage, and patience to become successful. Most people fail on the road to success and never achieve success. It takes hard work and years of dedication to reach success. Some people just get lucky and find success overnight but that is rare and is the exception rather than the rule. The slow and steady way of becoming rich is safe because it is done in a well-planned manner. Passive income is built up over time rather in an instant and that makes it a stable foundation for growth. Getting

MONEY GROWS ON TREES

rich overnight probably means you will lose everything you have overnight as well. It takes time to create value and to build up momentum that achieves success. If you create multiple channels of revenue, these will build up over time and each will become an Active Revenue Channel (ARC). You have to build up your ARC through patience and hard work but it is the foundation of the system that you are learning. The ARC System has the advantage of creating multiple channels of revenue from multiple sources. You create multiple streams of revenue that build up your net worth over time. For example, your first ARC could be your job, your second ARC could be your weekend gig DJ'ing parties, your 3rd ARC could be your off-work investing in stocks, your 4th ARC could be your weekend consulting

MONEY GROWS ON TREES

position for businesses, and so forth. The more Active Revenue Channels you create, the more money you will make. The average millionaire has 7 or more Active Revenue Channels that make them money. It is obviously impossible to take on more Active Revenue Channels than you can manage, but you have to stay focused on the idea that Active Revenue Channels increase your profitability. Active Revenue Channels fuel your growth and they allow you to Grow Rich over time. There are many popular forms of Active Revenue Channels and they include Real Estate as well as Stock Market Investing. The merits of Real Estate are well known which is why Real Estate is a preferred investment vehicle for investors seeking safe and steady passive income. Why are some start-ups successful and why

MONEY GROWS ON TREES

do some start-up companies fail? A start-up company seeks to grow to become a "unicorn" or a start-up whose valuation is worth more than $1,000,000,000. Start-ups share similar starts but there trajectory changes due to several factors including business model, future value of target market, leadership style, type, and their solvency. The Internet has featured scores of failed start-ups that featured an unworkable or un-profitable business model. Many of the first Internet start-ups had their business plans and related business model scribbled out on a napkin. Venture capitalists were quick to put their funds in to anything Internet related but quickly learned that not all business models are equal. Failed start-ups featured business models that spent more in customer acquisition costs than

MONEY GROWS ON TREES

generated revenue. The Future Value of a Target Market (FVTM) cannot always be calculated. Many start-ups found success in a trial and error manner because the market they were seeking to dominate did not exist. The start-ups were founded to create a product when the "critical mass" of buyers did not exist to justify a venture capital investment. Customer acquisition costs are obligatory especially when the market must be created for the product. The leadership style of the start-up will determine their future success. A disruptive type of start-up can reap great benefits as start-up Uber has experienced. Complimentary types of start-ups are also successful because they act as enablers for that specific industry. Solvency has always been a goal for all start-ups. Start-ups have

MONEY GROWS ON TREES

high cash burn rates causing their venture capital funders anxiety. The faster that a start-up reaches solvency, the sooner the shareholders can be rewarded for their investment. Too many Internet start-ups had to shut down operations because their revenue could not match their intensively high cash burn rate. Spending vital funds on items that do not add value to the customer is not intelligent and burns through a start-up's reserves. By viewing factors such as a start-up's business model, future value of target market, leadership style, type, and their solvency, a venture capitalist will better understand if that start-up is a viable investment. Billionaire Meg Whitman and film producer Jeffrey Katzenberg raised 1.7 Billion Dollars in 2020 and started a video streaming service for mobile

MONEY GROWS ON TREES

phones. They hired 250 people. The service shut down after 6 months. The question is whether it should have started in the first place. Why was this service needed? Quibi, as Katzenberg loved to say, was a me-too business. Instagram Reels already existed. Tik Tok already existed. YouTube. Netflix. Hulu. Why was this service needed? Why did they need 1.7 Billion Dollars? To buy new content? Surely they could have figured out this problem in the initial stages of planning the company. One Billion and seven hundred million dollars is larger than the Gross Domestic Product of many nations on earth. Quibi was a me-too and was not really offering anything that could be deemed innovative or novel. One of the secrets of making money is preserving time. When you outsource a task, you

MONEY GROWS ON TREES

are saving yourself time. When you outsource a task, you are conserving resources and saving money. You could try to do everything yourself but you are not a specialist in everything. You would produce low quality work is some things while producing high quality work in other things. You would be inconsistent because it would be impossible for you to try to do everything yourself. If you outsource your tasks or your work, you were able to save your energy for other tasks. Routine and mundane tasks such as graphic design, marketing, and public relations can be outsourced. Many things that you need can be outsourced, saving you money and time that can be spent in better ways. There are some people that like to do everything themselves. They see it as a badge of honor and as a sign of their productivity.

MONEY GROWS ON TREES

If you try to do everything yourself you will end up with mediocre or poor results. One of the first things that you have to do when you start your business is to check your ego. The days of huge overhead expenses and huge offices are done. The virtual company with outsourced services is the norm. Nike is one of the world's largest shoes manufacturers and they do not own a single factory. They outsource the production of their athletic shoes and they outsource many other vital services they use. Outsourcing has, in the past, received a negative image. Companies realized that they had to operate leaner and more efficiently while saving money. Outsourcing was the answer and it worked better than they had expected. Car companies moved to Mexico, Tech jobs moved to India, and other

MONEY GROWS ON TREES

industries quickly followed suit. Outsourcing created more value for the end customer because it prevented prices from being raised dramatically on various goods and services. Companies that don't outsource will face stiff competition from their rivals that do. Just as businesses have a credit and people have a personal credit history, people also have a human credit history. Loans are not always available through Banks and individuals are sometimes the only people that can lend you money for a business or real estate investment. Humans do trust each other if they have familial relations and they do lend large amounts of money to each other without consulting any lender, lending company, or bank. The Human Credit industry may not be an industry in the traditional sense of the term, but it does exist.

MONEY GROWS ON TREES

Cousins lend each other $200,000 at a time without any paperwork or promissory notes being exchanged. Humans provide capital to each other without any intermediary all the time and they do not have to even know each other. P2P Lending or Person to Person Lending is not new, but it is relatively new to the online world. P2P Lending exchanges are intermediaries that function as a marketplace for loan seekers and individual lenders. It is important to build up a track record of ethical business practices that give you a good reputation and enhance your likeability. It is a huge factor that is underestimated as it assumed that all lending and financing has been based on numbers. There are instances of loan seekers showing up to a Bank and asking for hundreds of millions of dollars

MONEY GROWS ON TREES

in loans based on a few press clippings in major newspapers. If it has worked for them, then it can work for you. A positive public image is essential to business operations and loan seekers have used Image Projection (showing yourself in a good way) successfully to attract major investors. There are many instances in which a traditional loan cannot be acquired and it is required to leverage reputation to achieve the results you are seeking. If you have a track record of paying back personal loans and maintaining your personal credit with people you have borrowed money from, they will be willing to loan you larger amounts at a later date. Raising capital person to person becomes easier when you have familial relations with them as well as demonstrating that you are responsible

MONEY GROWS ON TREES

when it comes to paying back their money. Un-ethical business conduct and "burning bridges" results in weakening your network of individuals that can assist you on your path to success. Your network can raise your net worth if you are able to build relationships and foster them in a mutually beneficial manner. But that depends on always paying back the person or business you have loaned from. A lawyer is a consultant in regards to legal matters. An accountant is a consultant in regards to financial numbers. They are worth every penny they are paid because they have insight and advanced in-depth knowledge regarding legal and financial matters. You should call a Lawyer and call an Accountant before every business decision. They may see something that

MONEY GROWS ON TREES

you do not. Three heads are better than
one. It is better to have a legal opinion
on a business matter than to face legal
proceedings. Lawyers like to joke that
life is better lived than litigated, and they
are right. A good lawyer is the difference
between your success and your defeat.
A good lawyer will show you the best
way to win with the least path of
resistance. An accountant can find
discrepancies in the numbers and can
give you concrete recommendations
that can save you time and money. An
accountant can also give you
recommendations that will prevent you
from making an investment that will
result in you losing your money.
Lawyers and accountants are
specialized in their respective fields and
their paid advice can help you progress
faster and in a safer manner. A business

MONEY GROWS ON TREES

investment should be viewed and analyzed by both an accountant as well as a lawyer. A legal perspective can help shape your business direction as well as protect your investment. Many lawyers are also certified public accountants (CPA), and this gives them greater in-sight and advanced knowledge about both legal and financial matters. It is common sense to do it but many people don't subscribe to common sense. Before you make an investment in real estate or a business, make sure you have both an experienced lawyer and accountant analyze it. You will save yourself a lot of time and money and you will be able to make an informed decision.

Debt Re-negotiation

MONEY GROWS ON TREES

Banks would rather re-negotiate their debts with customers than lose their customer because of a foreclosure. Mortgage debt and Business Loans can be re-negotiated with a Bank and it can be lowered substantially through negotiations. You can contact the bank holding the mortgage note or business loan, and re-negotiate the total amount of the loan as well as its terms (amortization, interest rate, etc.). Banks are opening to negotiating with customers and businesses that are in debt to them because it would be more costly for the customer or business to default on that loan. Debt can be re-negotiated and lowered substantially through a few phone calls and its rate and monthly payments can be lowered through negotiation. Even if your name is not on the mortgage note held by the

MONEY GROWS ON TREES

bank, you can offer to the seller of that property you are buying to have their debt re-negotiated with their bank. A mortgage broker, real estate agent, or lawyer, can re-negotiate debt for you and save you time. Debt re-negotiation is a standard practice in finance and it can result in saving you money in the short and long term. **Budgeting**

Even if your Active Revenue Channels generate 100 million dollars per year, you can still spend it frivolously if you do not budget. Every business, as well as every home, has to operate on a budget. If you are not cautious in your expenses you will see your profits wasted on activities that do no increase your sales or add value to the customer. You have to apply a budget and you have to stick to that budget to prevent

MONEY GROWS ON TREES

financial mis-management. If you are investing in a business that is a call center, is it important where they are located? Do they have to be located in a glitzy commercial office space that costs $50,000 per month or will a $2,000 per month warehouse suffice? Does every employee need a mobile phone that is paid for by the business? Does a business executive need to fly first class or will economy class be sufficient? Are the company executives holding expensive non-value adding company parties that add to the burn rate? Is the company pool table essential for transacting business? Is it the company's responsibility to spend $15,000 per month on stocking the fridge and providing free snacks? Are there too many executives in a company paying themselves high salaries? Is

MONEY GROWS ON TREES

there a need to buy XYZ raw material and pay exorbitant storage fees to store it for 6 months in order to manufacture finished goods today? Is it necessary to spend money on manufacturing when the business inventory is filled with un-sold goods? There are many areas in a business in which costs can be cut without sacrificing quality. Efficiency depends on reducing the waste in order to increase productivity (rate of output). Major businesses seek to invest in technology such as robotics to reduce costs while raising revenue. It should be the goal of all businesses to seek ways to reduce costs while increasing revenue through sales.

Marketing

MONEY GROWS ON TREES

Marketing is communication that creates brand awareness for your company. It makes the job of the sales person easier. It is easier to cold call decision makers when your brand is well known. An unknown brand has to go through the steps of educating their customer about their brand and its unique attributes. Marketing was viewed as advertising in the 1960's and these two terms were practically and functionally identical. Advertising is one element of marketing. It is important that you understand the various forms of marketing so that you are able to benefit from them. The types of Marketing include but are not limited to:

Affiliate Marketing – Paid Referrals to independent online marketers.

MONEY GROWS ON TREES

Cause Marketing – Representing the values of a cause (protect the environment) in your communications.

Chat Marketing – Live Chats that are hosted online with the purpose of interacting with potential or current customers.

Demo Marketing – Public demonstrations of the product or service at a location that has large amounts of foot traffic.

Direct Mail Marketing – Bulk Mail

Email Marketing – Bulk Email sent using an email list (usually a spreadsheet).

Endorsement Marketing – Paid Influencers that feature your product or service in return for payment.

MONEY GROWS ON TREES

Gift Marketing – Promotional gifts sent to key decision makers in corporations.

Guerrilla Marketing – Unorthodox style of marketing that uses stickers, wall posters, graffiti, and other means to broadcast a message.

In-Flight Marketing – Advertisements inside airline magazines or in airplanes.

Mobile Marketing – Bulk SMS/Text that is sent to mobile phones of potential or current customers.

Outdoor Marketing – Billboards and bus stop advertisements.

Radio Marketing – Short Radio Ads featured before and after TV shows.

Referral Marketing – Pay customers a commission for referrals.

MONEY GROWS ON TREES

Research Marketing – Research marketing is the use of surveys to discover customer buying habits. Questions are posed to potential customers about various products or services. The answers are analyzed and recommendations are made based on that information.

Social Media Marketing - Online

Television Marketing – TV Ads

Trade Show Marketing – Exhibitions are an important method for marketing your products and services to global buyers.

Transit Marketing – Advertisements on or inside moving vehicles including busses, trains, cars, and other transportation.

MONEY GROWS ON TREES

Viral Marketing – Word of Mouth

Voice Marketing – Podcasts, sound clips, and audio streams.

Promotional Marketing - Promotional marketing has many forms and they include (but are not limited to):

Coupons – Coupons are a popular way of attracting bargain buyers seeking discounts.

Free Stuff – People love getting promotional items and companies give away millions of branded pens, t-shirts, stickers, bags, and various gifts to potential and current customers each year. Trade shows are a popular location that companies use to give away promotional items.

MONEY GROWS ON TREES

Free Trial – Free trials are offered to use the product or service for free and to pay if they are satisfied.

Loyalty Programs – Loyalty cards and Member ID numbers are issued to each customer, allowing them to earn points and get discounts in the future. Loyalty programs have been used successfully by airlines as well as grocery supermarket chains to understand the buying trends among customers and to create customer loyalty.

Giveaways – Contests or sweepstakes excite potential and current customers. Giveaways entice potential customers to enter in order to win an item. The potential customers provide the business with their information, allowing that business to market and sell to those potential customers at a future date.

MONEY GROWS ON TREES

Sales

There are many forms of marketing, but the ultimate goal of marketing is the creation of sales. Marketing makes your job easier and makes the sales process smoother. Just as it is important for you to have understanding of Marketing, it is important for you to understand the various forms of Selling and they include (but are not limited to):

Business Development – Corporate partnerships with companies that agree to sell your products/services.

Channel Sales – Finding retail resellers to sell your products/services to end users. Channel Sales is a very powerful sales method because it leverages the already existing network of retailer to re-sell your products and services. Sales can increase exponentially using channel sales.

Demo Sales – Sales from a booth that is publicly demonstrating a product or service.

Direct Sales – Making cold or warm calls to potential customers with the purpose of making them a customer. Also known as Telemarketing or Outbound Sales.

Door to Door Sales – The oldest form of selling is door to door sales. It was direct selling before there was phone direct sales. Many major businesses grew through targeted door to door sales to homes and businesses.

E-Commerce Sales – Sales generated from an online store such as selling on Amazon.

MONEY GROWS ON TREES

Infomercials – Effective television selling method that uses long advertisements, 30 to 40 minutes in length, to generate responses from potential customers, leading to an inbound phone call sale.

You have to understand the 4 types of buyers and what motivates them to purchase.

Convenience Buyer – The convenience buyer purchases a product or service because of the purchasing ease. They are motivated by the ease of purchasing the product as a solution, rather than by the product itself. A buyer of online food delivery services is most likely a convenience buyer. A buyer of online groceries is most likely a convenience buyer.

MONEY GROWS ON TREES

Price Buyer – The price buyer is motivated by hunting for bargains and finding the lowest price possible. Many consumer electronics companies started out by appealing to price buyers, by undercutting their competitors on price. A buyer of a Low Cost Budget Airline ticket is most likely a price buyer. A buyer that purchases food at the 99 Cents Store is most likely a Price Buyer.

Brand Buyer – The brand buyer is motivated by status and symbols that project an image for its user. The brand buyer is not motivated by price or convenience, and will pay a premium price and experience in-convenience (wait in lines) in order to acquire the desired product or service. A buyer of an Apple iPhone is most likely a Brand Buyer.

MONEY GROWS ON TREES

Value Buyer – The value buyer is motivated by receiving the most value for the least amount paid. They are interested in receiving the greatest value for the purchase they are making. A buyer of a Toyota automobile is most likely a Value Buyer.

Knowing what motivates your customers make the job of selling to them much easier. Selling to your customers is the lifeline of your company. Every department should exist to support the Sales department and their selling efforts. Sales define a company's Profit and Loss statement and they result in a healthy Balance Sheet. Sales efforts should define all of the operations of a company and should lead the company's other departments. If you are afraid of selling, then you must hire people that can sell for you. Everything you do is a sales job. In investing, you are selling a business on why they should take your investment rather than that of your competitor. When you buy an owner financed home, you are selling the Seller as to the reasons that they should sell the house to you. It doesn't feel like Sales and it doesn't necessarily have to. All Revenue Generation occurs by Sales and it is by far the most important function of your company and it is the function in which you should invest the most time and effort. Sales fuels human resources and sales fuel the dollars that the marketing department uses to communicate the brand. It is important to understand the steps involved in direct selling. As CEO, you may tell yourself that you are not a Salesperson, but you will be surprised to

MONEY GROWS ON TREES

find out that the CEO's of companies
are the top salesperson in their
organization because they are out
meeting with other CEO's and forming
alliances. Even the CEO is a
salesperson because they are selling
the brand values of that organization to
a wider audience. Everything comes
down to sales and there are many
instances of organizations shutting
down because of one or two major sales
accounts being lost. A major shipbuilder
that loses out on a five hundred million
dollar order could risk having to
downsize or shut down. A major
commercial airplane manufacturer that
loses a key order could end up having to
downsize. Lost sales has huge
consequences for a company and those
consequences can include bankruptcy,
downsizing, closing departments, and

MONEY GROWS ON TREES

scaling operations. Lost sales through customer switching or lost sales through high attrition, can break a business and cause it to re-organize. Each sales call does cost you time and money, which is why you should prepare beforehand before contacting a potential customer. What it is that you want to say? What do you want the result of this phone call to be? Do you want to move the forward one step closer to a sale on this call or are you are seeking to get the customer to pay on this call? If you plan beforehand the flow of the call and rehearse it in your mind or on paper, you will be better able to achieve the results you are seeking. Picture yourself in your mind closing the call with success and reaching the outcome you are seeking. Understand your motives before making the call and you will be able to easily understand the direction the call should be going in.

Sales Steps

Introduction – Make a simple introduction and introduce your company and yourself.

Discover Decision maker(s) – You have to discover the names of the key decision maker(s) that are responsible for purchasing what you are selling.

Qualifications – How much does the buyer buy per year? What problems are they facing that you could provide a solution for? Are they the sole decision-maker?

In Person/Online/Phone Presentation – Give a presentation on the product or service you are selling. Include a proposal if necessary.

Handling Objections – Answer any questions they have. Each question is a concern in the form of a question. Handle their concerns by answering their questions. An objection is really a request for more information on the part of the buyer. Inability to properly handle objections from a potential customer could result in you losing the sale and losing the customer permanently.

Closing – You have to ask for their business and for them to buy from you. There are various ways to close a sale and they include writing up the order, the pros and cons comparison, and asking for their business.

MONEY GROWS ON TREES

Writing Up The Order is as simple as filling out the printed or online order form that completes the sale and asking questions from the customer to fill in the fields to complete the order. Ask them how they would like to pay and lead them to payment. Writing Up The Order is a linear closing technique that leads the buyer from introduction to the close. A bookseller in a bookstore asks what the customer wants, provides them with a solution, and then leads them to the cash register. It is a linear closing technique. Pros and Cons Comparison is a very simple yet effective closing technique whereby you use a piece of paper or image to convey the pros (positives) about buying your product or service versus the cons (negatives) about buying your product or service. The Pros and Cons Comparison is a

MONEY GROWS ON TREES

powerful closing technique that provides a visual to the customer and better helps them understand the benefits of buying your product or service. Asking For Their Business is a closing technique that has the Seller ask the Buyer to buy from them based on the presentation you have delivered. It is a logical and practical close that uses a straightforward statement to close the sale.

Conditions

Conditions affect your sale and they can prevent you from moving forward in your sale. Sales conditions are not an objection or a request for more information about your products or services. Conditions that prevent the sale must be recorded by the seller so that the seller can re-visit the buyer

MONEY GROWS ON TREES

when the condition(s) have passed. The first condition is if all the decision makers are not present to make a decision together. Another condition is that the decision to purchase may be made by a group of individuals that meet 3 times per year and their next meeting is 3 months away, causing you to have to delay the sale for 3 months. Another condition is that their current budget is not enough to purchase your product. There are a myriad of conditions that affect sales and prevent you from moving forward. A condition is different than an objection, which is just a request for more information. A condition is a real reason why the sale cannot move forward currently. Whether you personally sell or you have salespersons working for you, it is important to have understanding of sales so that it can help increase your revenue. No product sells itself except a commodity like gasoline. Gasoline sells itself because an automobile or a motorcycle cannot work without it. Because gasoline is a commodity, it cannot be branded like a shoe company brand. Electricity is a utility (electricity can be considered a commodity) and it therefore cannot be branded like a luxury men's clothing brand. A brand does not just sell itself. Whether if it is a product or service, it has to be sold. Even if you are IBM or Honda or Caterpillar or Samsung, the salespersons sell their products (or services) in a pro-active (rather than passive) manner. Nothing just sells itself. Everything has to be sold and salespersons are a company's most important corporate asset because they are the driver of its revenue growth. Without sales, a company has nothing. It is not enough to exist as a company. A company has to drive sales resulting in income generation. Income generation is the purpose of sales and increasing sales volume will allow a business to grow.

Raising Capital

Raising capital provides you necessary funds for investing in real estate and business.

There are various ways to raise capital for investment and they include:

Friends/Family – People tend to over-look friends and family but they are the easiest persons to talk to about investing with you.

MONEY GROWS ON TREES

Angel Investors – Angel investors are individuals with a high net worth that are seeking to increase their net worth through investing in start-up companies. Angel investors tend to be less experienced than institutional venture capitalists but they are easier to approach (and sometimes to work with!). Angel investors take more risks than venture capitalists and are generally more approachable.

Venture Capitalists – Venture Capitalists are investors tied to a firm of investors. VC companies or VC firms have experienced specialized investors with advanced knowledge in various fields such as tech.

Hard Money Lenders – Hard money lenders used collateral to loan money.

MONEY GROWS ON TREES

Also known as Secured Loans or Collateralized Loans.

Banks – Banks create business lines of credit for companies and can arrange equipment financing. Banks require business line of credit applicants to have higher levels of credit.

Crowd-funding – Many start-up companies found their first funding through the use of online crowd-funding websites.

Customers – Customers can provide capital through a Pre-Order Sale.

Top 10 Reasons Businesses Succeed (In no particular order)

1. The business met a real need.

MONEY GROWS ON TREES

2. A demand existed for the service or good.

3. The business was able to sell their goods or services at a lower price.

4. The business had outstanding customer service.

5. The business maintained good relations within the community.

6. The business didn't reduce quality and dramatically raise prices once they achieved a following.

7. The business had employees that went above and beyond the norm in providing service.

8. The business provided services or goods of a higher quality than their competitors.

9. The business advertised heavily.

10. The business created value through providing its goods or services.

**Top 10 Reasons Businesses Fail
(In no particular order)**

1. Goods or services were of a poor quality.

2. Goods or services were too high priced.

MONEY GROWS ON TREES

3. Business was antagonistic towards local community.

4. Business provided poor customer service.

5. Business failed to create and distribute effective advertising.

6. Business didn't create value for customers.

7. Business had poorly trained employees.

8. Lack of demand for the business's goods or services.

9. The business didn't meet a real need.

MONEY GROWS ON TREES

10. The business raised prices
    dramatically and/or reduced
    quality after achieving a following.

Sometimes you have to be spontaneous
in business. Some businesspersons
have nothing prepared beforehand.
They improvise and make ad hoc
decisions until they reach their goal.
Being adventurous is all about
impromptu business decision making.
Going in to a situation without
preparation purposefully in order to have
a flexible and negotiable position. In
some situations, such as business
negotiations, this is a useful stance to
take. A flexible position will benefit you
while a rigid position will hurt your
competitor. It is impossible to predict
with any degree of certainty if you will be
successful in one thing or another. You

MONEY GROWS ON TREES

have to be commercially flexible to new business ideas. A business idea without execution is not worth much at all. If you want to attract Angel Investors or Venture Capitalists to invest in your business, then it has to be more than an idea. It has to be a functional business. Even if the business is losing money, it is a functioning business. A business idea is nothing at all. It is an idea that has not been executed. It is an idea that has not been practically tested or applied. Throwing out ideas is for brainstorming in a meeting. Executing the operations of a business are what businesses do and what businesses are about. Sitting and dreaming of an idea would be a waste of your time if you do not implement the necessary steps to make the idea in to a working money generating business. Creating new

MONEY GROWS ON TREES

businesses that align with your core business will allow you to have greater growth. Investing in up and coming start-up companies that will bring a benefit to your core business will allow your core business to grow.

Mining Claims

My Grandfather was an oilman. My Father was an oilman. They spent their lives chasing oil services contracts and partnered with many major oil services companies including BJ Hughes. There are many people that sit and hope that crude oil will disappear. 100 years strong. The world is still dependent on crude oil and will continue to be dependent on crude oil for the next 100

MONEY GROWS ON TREES

years. There is no such thing as electric motor 300 person passenger planes. You may be able to haul 4 people with electric power, but you will not be able to fly 300 persons for 12 hours straight on electric power. Oil is not going anywhere. There are over 10 million persons in the United States that receives royalties from crude oil located on their land. By owning the Mineral Rights on their land, they are able to contract with oil exploration companies that pay a small fee to the landowner to explore the land. The fee is usually small, around $500. If the oil exploration company finds oil or gas on the land, they then sign a contract with the landowner to exploit the natural resources on that land. As the landowner owns the Mineral Rights to that land, the landowner receives

MONEY GROWS ON TREES

approximately 20 to 25 percent royalties on the oil produced on the land. All oil wells deplete over time because the oil they are pumping out depletes, but they are usually capped off between 30 to 50 years after the start of exploitation. An oil rig costs anywhere from 5 million to 20 million dollars to purchase. An oil drilling team costs $50,000 per day to operate. The costs are enormous, the oil drilling company pays the costs, and the landowner doesn't have to pay anything at all. The landowner owns the Mineral Rights to the land and can contract with oil and gas companies to explore for oil and gas and to pay royalties in order to exploit the natural resources. The landowner wins big without having to invest anything in order to receive royalties. The landowner did the investing when they purchased land that

MONEY GROWS ON TREES

potentially contained oil and gas on it.
Mining claims can also be purchased for
Gold placer and Gold lode mining sites.
In this scenario, you would purchase the
Mineral Rights to a certain land and then
you would contract to a mining company
on a 50/50 percentage split to exploit
the natural resources. The mining
company would pay for the operation of
the mine and its teams in order to
receive the 50 percent royalty. You as
the landowner allow the mining
company to operate the mine in return
for 50 percent of all the Gold (or
precious metals) recovered. A 50/50
split is a legitimate offer in a landowner-
mining company arrangement. An
unpatented mining claim is a mining
claim where you only own the Mineral
Rights to the land but you do not own
the land. A patented mining claim is a

mining claim where you own the Mineral Rights and you own the land. Because placer mining is surface mining, an unpatented mining claim is more than sufficient. If the mining claim you wish to purchase or have purchased is perfect for lode mining, then a patented mining claim might be able to allow you to speed up paperwork and permits with the EPA, BLM, or other authorities.

Power of Compound Interest

There is a secret that many don't talk about but it has fueled investors, businesses, and banks coffers with riches. It is Compound Interest. If you are able to achieve 18 percent return a year on your money through investing in mutual funds, start-ups, miscellaneous financial investments, you will be able to grow your money exponentially over 20

MONEY GROWS ON TREES

years. 20 years seems like a long time doesn't it? 20 years is a short period of time. 20 years comes and goes like it was 1 year or 5 years. Time doesn't stop for you or anyone. Time keeps moving. Why not let time make you money? If you are able to invest $50,000 in a business that gives you a steady 18 percent a year return on your money, and you are able to put that return back on your original money, then you will earn compound interest. $50,000 receiving a steady 18 percent a year with its return put back on your money, will give you over 2 million United States Dollars in 20 years. What? That is right. $50,000 invested in a compound interest account for 20 years will transform in to 2 million US dollars. This is one of the secrets of making money. Using time to win and

MONEY GROWS ON TREES

using compound interest to grow. Every money that is generated is re-invested on top of the principal you had originally invested. This creates momentum. This creates a snowball effect. The power of compound interest is in time and re-investing. As the amount grows larger, so does the return. Compound Interest builds on itself because the money generated annually is re-invested back on top of the principal. If you use this secret of making money, then you will absolutely win and grow. You have to have the discipline to live within your means and to re-invest everything back on top of the principal. If you are able to have the discipline to do this, then you will grow stronger and richer safely over 20 years. Use the power of compound interest to make you money and to make you win. Compound interest, other

MONEY GROWS ON TREES

than real estate and gold, is the safest way to grow steadily rich over time. It will take time. 20 years. It will take discipline. You have to live within your means and you have to re-invest everything that you get back on top of your principal.

Accept Your Flaws

No one is perfect. Everyone has flaws and qualities that they are un-happy about. Just as you would promote your strengths you should also learn to accept your flaws. You should learn to accept other people's flaws as well. If you become so judgmental that everyone around has to be perfect, then you will soon find yourself alone. If you promote an atmosphere that is not flexible to human error, then you will find your employees and independent

MONEY GROWS ON TREES

contractors making every attempt to hide their mistakes rather than to deal with them openly. This will hurt your business financially. You have to be accepting of human error and mistakes in order to deal with the problems they create. You have to accept the flaws inherent in yourself and in your team in order to move past them. Being rigid creates a company culture that is not conducive to change. Your company and your core business may have to change over time and being inflexible will cause your business to fail. Try to be less judgmental about everything and you will find yourself finding new solutions to old problems. As long as you are flexible and open to human error, you can train your team to deal with the errors as they are created.

MONEY GROWS ON TREES

Reputation of Honesty

It may take 5, 10, or 20 years, but eventually you will be recognized as a trustworthy honest individual if you never cheat and steal from anyone else. Sometimes, scoundrels and villains are celebrated, to the detriment of the earth. In your case, as long as you live a trustworthy life that involves never stealing from anyone else, you will be recognized as a trustworthy individual. This might not mean a whole lot to you. You may ask yourself "Who cares if I am trustworthy"? Many entrepreneurs and important business persons value trust as being among the most important qualities they look for in an individual. In a world of un-trustworthy people, it is very refreshing to meet or re-join with a trustworthy person. Humans have a

MONEY GROWS ON TREES

record, that may or may not be written down, but this record forms their reputation. A person with a trustworthy reputation is invested in and given money to manage. Too many times, un-trustworthy persons have been given important money management roles and they have failed in their duties. A trustworthy person brings a lot to the table. A trustworthy person brings character and fortitude and honesty to the table. That is worth billions of dollars to an entrepreneur. That is worth billions of dollars to a CEO. That is worth billions of dollars to an investor. Money is not the only thing of value in a transaction. Reputation is of high value in a financial transaction and a transaction without this reputation can create problems such as theft. A reputation of honesty comes from doing

MONEY GROWS ON TREES

the right thing for many years until you are recognized as a person that possesses a character that is trustworthy. An un-trustworthy individual with a Power of Attorney from you could wreak havoc on your finances and put you in a precarious situation. An un-trustworthy person with a Power of Attorney from you could put you in debt and financial misery for many years. Until you have felt the pain and anguish of transacting business with an un-trustworthy person, you will not be aware of the worth and value of a trustworthy person. A trustworthy person is worth more than money because money can be re-produced but a trustworthy person cannot. They either exist or they don't, but they cannot be printed or re-produced like paper money on a printing machine.

MONEY GROWS ON TREES

Be Inventive

New money is created when a new source of income generation is created. A new source of income generation is a new source of funding for research and development to create new products. A chess playing machine known as the Turk Automaton was invented by Hungarian nobleman Baron Wolfgang Von Kemplen in 1769. The Turk Automaton was a chess playing machine that was presented to and demonstrated for princes and potentates throughout Europe. The Turk

The Turk Automaton beat Napoleon in a game of Chess.

MONEY GROWS ON TREES

Automaton beat the best chess players in the world and even played against Napoleon Bonaparte. Charles Babbage, the father of the modern computer, was inspired to create calculating machines because of it and the modern scientific and literary greats like Edgar Allen Poe wrote about its workings. Poe said "The Turk plays with his left hand. All the movements of the arm are at right angles. In this manner, the hand (which is gloved and bent in a natural way,) being brought directly above the piece to be moved, descends finally upon it, the fingers receiving it, in most cases, without difficulty. Occasionally, however, when the piece is not precisely in its proper situation, the Automaton fails in his attempt at seizing it. When this occurs, no second effort is made, but

MONEY GROWS ON TREES

the arm continues its movement in the direction originally intended, precisely as if the piece were in the fingers." When it was demonstrated for the first time, individuals in attendance were in near shock as a machine was able to beat the finest players in the world in Chess. Many theories were created about its workings and much writing was done

 Microsoft was founded in 1975.

speculating as to how it operated. Many believed that there was a man hidden inside the machine that allowed the machine to think and move the pieces. If this were so, the individual would have to have been a midget so as to be able to fit in to the machine. But even if this

MONEY GROWS ON TREES

theory were true, where would you find a chess playing midget that was able to defeat the best chess players in the world? The other theory was that it was purely mechanical movements with the illusion of intelligence. The machine was mostly likely pure automata, an invention that was based around the movements of gears, wires, and pulleys. But the creation of a machine, at that time, was considered so fantasy-like that people were in near shock when witnessing it for the first time. If even it was purely a machine, how could a machine defeat the greatest chess players in Europe in the late 1700's? What advanced technologies were being used that allowed for this? The Turk Automaton was stored in a museum that burned down, destroying the machine forever. Imitations of the

MONEY GROWS ON TREES

machine were created later but the original technology that Von Kemplen created was never seriously analyzed other than through observations of individuals watching the demonstrations. Von Kemplen was an extraordinary and gifted inventor of unusual creations. His Turk Automaton not only created a stir but also advanced the study of automata creation, mostly importantly inspiring Charles Babbage's computing machines. There is an ongoing problem occurring in large and small corporations, whether member run or board run. The problem revolves around a lack of vision in product development. Of course larger companies take longer to make decisions and have to expend much more resources in contrast to smaller companies.

MONEY GROWS ON TREES

Money Has Rules

1. Never invest in a business or financial vehicle that you do not directly control. If the ship sinks and in business it often does, you will be angry and you will play the blame game. If the business wins, you will win. If the business fails, there is a lack of accountability and your investment disappears.

2. Never make an un-collateralized loan. If someone wants to borrow money from you, then they must present some form of collateral that is financially viable. If someone wants to borrow money from you then they should provide something of value that

MONEY GROWS ON TREES

you could sell to recover your
money.

3. Gold has been a traditionally safe
    investment that has risen in value
    steadily over the past 100 years.
    There is a reason why all Central
    Banks of every nation on earth
    invest their money in Gold
    bullion. Gold cannot be
    reproduced in contrast to paper
    money which can be printed.
    Gold is scarce and valuable. The
    price of Gold is uniform and it is a
    tradable commodity.

4. Real Estate has been a
    traditionally safe investment that
    has risen in value steadily over
    the past 100 years. Most people
    that are millionaires became so

through the acquisition and sale
of real estate.

5. Investing in a business you will
    start and operate is great and
    adventurous. Just understand
    that 90 percent of startup
    businesses fail in the first year.

6. Money loses value over time
    which is why money is invested in
    financial vehicles that have
    higher and higher rates of return.

7. Friendship and business are two
    different things. Don't ruin
    friendship in order to force
    businesses to start.

MONEY GROWS ON TREES

8. Money is not an end to itself. Money is a means to provide safety, security, and happiness.

9. Money should be never be trapped in low producing financial vehicles.

10. There is no logic that could provide financial predictions. All investments are speculations.

The Pareto Rule or the 80/20 Rule is that 80 percent of your income will be generated from 20 percent of your customers, is still true most of the time. The point is to create as many Active Revenue Channels as you are able to invest time in to and manage. Passive Income is income that is generated in a

MONEY GROWS ON TREES

passive manner but for you to achieve passive income you have to be active. You can't wait around for business to happen. You have to be the one that makes business happen. You have to be able to create new passive income revenue streams by chasing them as they will not fall from the sky and land in your lap. If you are motivated to make money and you are willing to learn the MGOT system, then you will be successful (if you keep hammering away at it). The MGOT system depends on you creating Active Revenue Channels and using the money you generate from them in order to create more Active Revenue Channels. Active Revenue Channels cannot be wished in to existence or summoned using a Talisman or Incantations. Active Revenue Channels are created as an

MONEY GROWS ON TREES

active effort by an entrepreneur seeking to make money. The name of the game is make money, and passive income revenue streams (Active Revenue Channels) will allow you to generate the funds required to create growth. Active Revenue Channels have to be built up one step at a time. The 1000 mile road begins with one step is an old yet wise saying. You cannot build an Active Revenue Channel unless you take the steps involved. Let us take the example of buying owner financed properties in order to create an Active Revenue Channel. You have to spend hundreds of hours searching through newspapers, online ads, and other media outlets in order to create a list of properties that are worth buying. Let us say you put in 14 hours finding real estate properties in one week. That would be a little over

MONEY GROWS ON TREES

two and a half hours a day. Out of 24
hours in a day, 2 hours a day is
approximately $1/12^{th}$ of your day. In that
14 hours you put in, in one week, you
are able to create a list of potential real
estate properties to purchase. In that
one week, you find 10 properties worth
buying. After doing your own due
diligence, you discover that 4 of them
have serious structural problems that
excludes you from buying them
(because they would require far too high
expenses to fix). The remaining 6
properties, you place offers on. From
the 6 properties you placed offers on,
you were able to enter sales negotiation
with 1 who finally agrees to sell you the
property. The property is $50,000 and
the owner that is financing the property
to you asks for a 20 percent down
payment of $10,000. You don't have

MONEY GROWS ON TREES

$10,000, but you have $5,000 that you saved up (hopefully). You offer the owner $5,000 in cash for half of the down payment with the remaining $5,000 of the down payment to be amortized and added to your monthly payments to the seller of the property. Since the owner of the property that is financing the sale of the property to you is seeking cash, you offer some cash for the down payment or you can ask all of the down payment be amortized. Creative financing depends on you being able to find multiple ways to purchase a property with minimal or no down payment. Passive income is best generated through real estate and it is why it is the focus of the MGOT system. Seller financing is standard practice in business and more so in real estate. Any search on Google will yield

MONEY GROWS ON TREES

thousands of websites that are advertising Owner Financed Properties. From $1,000 land for sale to $50,000,000 multi-family apartment complexes, with a simple search you can find owner financed properties being marketed daily. Every property is going to have some type of problem. The problem could be cosmetic and fixed with a few buckets of paint or the problem could be structural requiring a considerable expense. It is your duty to completely do your research and conduct due diligence, which means you have to not only view paperwork but you have to be willing to visit the various real estate properties and inspect them personally. It is impossible to understand the condition of a property without viewing it. If you are going to invest money in real estate, it is a good

MONEY GROWS ON TREES

idea to attempt to see it firsthand. What if the staircase looks good in the picture but in functionality, the staircase is near collapsing? Are you willing to get sued because the staircase collapsed in the 2 bedroom owner financed property you just purchased? Close inspection can reveal cosmetic as well as structural problems that exist or that might occur in the future. Unless you do a walk through and turn on the water pipes for example, how will you know if you have leaking or broken pipes? The property has to be tested and these are the various items that you should be check:

Piping – Old piping can be replaced or upgraded.

Electricity – Electrical wiring can be replaced or upgraded.

MONEY GROWS ON TREES

Heating/Cooling Systems – Heating and Cooling systems can be repaired or replaced.

Water/Fire Damage – Insulation and new walling can be installed.

Cosmetic Damages – Painting and polishing.

Structural Integrity – Broken columns, missing floorboards, etc can be upgraded or replaced.

Roofing – Roofing can be replaced or upgraded.

All owner financed properties require small to large level remodeling. It is your duty to conduct due diligence by

MONEY GROWS ON TREES

inspecting the property and listing the problems that exist (or could exist). You should get quotations from multiple contractors as to the price and come up with a sum total amount in order to understand how much it will cost you to remodel the owner financed property you will be purchasing. Every property requires your investment in order for it to become rentable and/or sellable. Of course you could make a healthy profit by fixing and flipping homes, but the purpose of the MGOT system is for you to create Active Revenue Channels instead of one time profits. An Active Revenue Channel that I have discussed several times in Grow Rich was Owner Financed Properties. The point of purchasing owner financed properties is to remodel them, re-finance them, and rent them out. You should be seeking to

MONEY GROWS ON TREES

acquire as many properties as possible and hold on to them rather than to buy them with the purpose of selling them. Every new property you acquire will create a new Active Revenue Channel for you. Imagine each Active Revenue Channel as a Tree that bears fruit, with the fruit representing money. You want to plant as many Trees as possible. The more Active Revenue Channels you possess, the greater the amount of fruit (money). Each Active Revenue Channel requires your motivation and enthusiasm. Each Active Revenue Channel requires you to invest your time and energy in to building them up until each one is viable and lucrative. Each Active Revenue Channel adds to your monthly income revenue generation allowing you to achieve greater growth in the future. Not all Active Revenue

MONEY GROWS ON TREES

Channels will perform as you expect them to. Some will under-perform and will require you to put in a greater amount of time for them to see results. Some Active Revenue Channels, like purchasing owner financed properties, give you greater results (more money). Since each Active Revenue Channel is a tree bearing fruit, you have to spend most of your time in searching for new Active Revenue Channels to create. In contrast to a one time profit that you make by fixing and flipping a home, buying an owner financed property allows you to create lifelong income through rentals. Rental properties create a healthy monthly income revenue that allows you to save up for buying more rental properties. Owner financed deals are not only available on traditional real estate such as apartments or

MONEY GROWS ON TREES

townhouses. Owner financed real estate includes raw agricultural land and forest land (private). If you purchased 1 acre of raw forest land that was heavily wooded for $1,000, you could sell the trees on that land to a forestry logging company for $1,500 to $5,000 per acre. They would get the trees, you would get your land cleared (prepared for construction) for free, and you would get a few thousand dollars. Money Grows On Trees. If you purchased an Acre of raw agricultural land for $5,000 and you planted fruit trees (oranges) on it, you would be able to recoup your investment in the first year. The land value would rise and you would profit from the fruits you sold. Money Grows On Trees. Everyone is so enthralled and mesmerized by the lure of investing in Big Tech that they forgot that Billionaire

MONEY GROWS ON TREES

Bill Gates is the largest farm landowner in the United States. What is good for the geese is good for the gander. The price of food has risen and continues to rise as more people move in to major cities. A simple reality exists that people don't want to live on farms anymore and they don't want to work in farms. They want to live and work in an urban or suburban environment in a major metropolitan city. Food prices keep rising as less people want to farm. It is a logical effect of supply and demand. There is a reason that billionaires are investing in farmland. Farmland is finite and food is finite. When each American consumes 5000 to 6000 calories per day and that means that a lot of food that has to be produced on a daily basis. McDonald's feeds 48 million persons per day (and this figure continues rising

MONEY GROWS ON TREES

daily). Considering that French Fries are the top selling item at McDonald's, that is an extraordinary amount of potatoes used per day. McDonald's surely makes money from selling French Fries, but the landowner makes money first. The first billionaires on earth were farmers. In many nations on earth, the richest persons are still landowners, specifically farmers. Any where there are persons, there are persons to be fed. Humans can go without having an office. Humans can go without having a car (as hundreds of millions of people in Europe understand). Humans cannot go without food. If you buy land for farming and grow oranges, for example, you can sell those oranges for money, you can trade those oranges for other commodities or finished products, and you squeeze those oranges and produce orange

MONEY GROWS ON TREES

juice. How large of a space would be needed to set up a bottling operation or canning production line? Very little space would be required and the production equipment, whether automated or semi-automated, would be minimal in comparison to the revenues you would generate. The first and most important thing you should do before you begin farming is to write a thorough business plan that answers key questions. What will you be growing, your organization and the responsibilities of each member, your market, and financials (gross revenue projection, expenses, etc). The more you plan out your future farming operation, the easier it will be to start and implement. No one is born a farmer. Farming is learned through first-hand experience and that means doing it

MONEY GROWS ON TREES

yourself in order to learn. There are various colleges and universities that teach farming, but theoretical knowledge is useless unless it is applied in the real world. You can only become a farmer by farming. All the courses in the world will not make you a farmer. Farming and gaining first-hand experience will make you a farmer. You might ask if farming is so great, then why aren't rich capitalists running towards farming. The rich capitalists in the United States started from farming and some returned to farming once they became rich in other industries. There must be a valid reason that one of the richest men on the earth, Bill Gates, is now the largest farm owner in the United States. Do you think you know more than Bill Gates? It is highly doubtful that you do. Bill Gates knows a lot that you or I don't. If Bill Gates is

MONEY GROWS ON TREES

heavily investing in farming and farm lands, then there must be value in it. Farming is not a dodgy Ponzi scheme venture like Crypto Currency. Farming is how we eat and farming is how we live. The world can live without digital money or digital social networks or digital exchanges. The world cannot live one day without food. Everything on earth would cease to exist and everything on earth would shut down, if the food supply on earth was affected for one day. If Crypto Currency doesn't exist, it makes no difference in anyone's life. I will continue purchasing things in United States dollars or in English Pounds or in Japanese Yen or in Chinese Yuan or in Silver Bars or using Gold Coins. Crypto currency is not vital to the operation of life on earth. It is a pastime for speculators and it is a hobby for passive

MONEY GROWS ON TREES

day traders. Gold is vital which is why every computer on earth has gold in it. If all crypto currency exchanges stopped tomorrow, it would not affect anything on earth the least bit. If farms stopped producing and selling food, the entire earth would be affected and it could lead to famine, starvation, and mass deaths. You can go without buying a Meme Crypto Currency. Can you go 2 days without food? Even if you were able to go 2 days without food, by Day 3 you would be completely energy-less and weak. By Day 5 of going without eating food, you would surely be hospitalized. Food is vital and that means farming and organic food production is vital to our existence. Everyone wants 1 million percent Return on Investment which is why they run to things like Crypto Currency. Sure, a few people got very

MONEY GROWS ON TREES

rich and many people lost money trying to get in. Whether people got rich or lost money on crypto currency, the undeniable reality is that the introduction of crypto currency in to society is directly responsible for the steep rise in inflation in the United States. Every new crypto currency token introduced reduces the worth of the United States Dollar as well as reducing the value of other fiat currencies globally. As new millionaires and billionaires are created globally from investing in crypto currencies, the owners of traditional assets (land owners and real estate owners) raise the prices of their real estate in order to compensate. Even consumer brands have been forced to raise their prices in order to keep up with the inflation. This has caused traditional fiat money to de-value and this forced real estate owners

MONEY GROWS ON TREES

to raise the prices of their real estate in order to not get left behind. Farmers in turn also raised the price of food, making investment in to farm lands more viable. Inflation is usually a chain reaction where sellers and producers raise their prices to compensate for the rise in real estate prices. If the sellers and producers didn't raise their prices, they would be unable to purchase more real estate. Any investor in anything, wishes to see some form of growth where sales increase. Even if sales increase, the prices still have to be raised by sellers and producers in order to compensate for the rise in real estate prices. Inflation is not a mysterious occurrence; inflation is a given reality that must be accepted. In order to hedge against inflation, you must become a producer that can raise the

MONEY GROWS ON TREES

prices of your goods and services in order to compensate for the inevitable and unfortunate rise in real estate prices. In any business you invest in, you have to compare the rates of your Return on Investment. Real estate, such as apartments or houses, usually give around 4 or 5 percent Return on Investment annually. 4 or 5 percent Return on Investment is hardly attractive to an investor and would not make sense if you wish to capture 10 percent or more Return on Investment. Farming provides that vehicle and allows you to achieve higher rates of Return on Investment. Farming gives you a higher rate of Return on Investment in comparison to buying traditional income property, but it is important to note that Farming Revenue is not passive (unless you are share cropping). Passive

MONEY GROWS ON TREES

Farming Revenue could be generated through purchasing a farm and then signing a 50/50 contract with a farming operator to work the land. If you have to personally stand on a farm and manage the farm, the income you will generate is not passive. You would have to put in time and do the work in order to see the results. If you buy a farm and decide to sign a 50/50 contract with a farmer, it would be passive income and you would be able to generate higher rates of Return on Investment than by personally working the farm yourself. The value is in the ownership of the farm as you could change the farming operator on your land several times until you arrive at one which satisfies your revenue expectations. You as the farm land owner are permanent but the farming operator will stay or go depending on

MONEY GROWS ON TREES

your satisfaction with their level of output. Let us say for example, that you purchase 20 Acres for growing tomatoes. After you purchase your property and go through all the legal registrations, you would seek out a farming operator to work the land on a 50/50 split contract. It is more than likely that if you buy farm land, there will be other farmers in a close proximity to that land you just purchased. You can contract with the farmers in close proximity to your farm, on a 50/50 split arrangement, to work your land. They already possess the experience and the knowledge to get the job done and you have the most important piece, which is the farm land. It is a myth that you have to start big. You can start with a small piece of land and buy larger pieces of land in the future in order to grow your

MONEY GROWS ON TREES

operation. You don't have to be located in a specific place as your job is managing over the revenue generation rather than working the land to generate produce. It would be better to purchase the farm lands in areas that are accessible to you or within a short distance. Unfortunately, this is not always possible. You may be in Los Angeles and your farm may be in the Central Valley of California or outside Sacramento. You would be 1 hour flight time away from your farm, not including the driving time required to visit the actual farm. Even if you were able to visit the farm regularly, you could use various forms of communication including Skype and Zoom, to see the actual results of the farming operator's work. You could receive daily, weekly, or monthly reports on farming output.

MONEY GROWS ON TREES

You would receive monthly revenue from the farming output and the monthly revenue would be the greatest indicator as to the success (or lack thereof) of the farming operator. Even if you visited your farm, once every three months, the monthly revenue would reveal the level of dedication and productivity of the farming operator working your land. You can change the farming operator if they are unable to satisfy your revenue expectations but the farming operator cannot just create more land. Land is finite and is unable to be created. As the farming land owner, you have the advantage because you can change the farming operator until you are satisfied with their level of revenue generation. You could try to farm yourself, but if you are not an experienced farmer with specialization in one or two or three

MONEY GROWS ON TREES

different crops, you could end up destroying your production crop resulting in little or no income for your farm. It is much wiser to generate passive income using a 50/50 split agreement to generate income from the existing land you have purchased (or are planning on purchasing). It is true that no one is born a farmer but the various experiences of a specialized experienced farmer are difficult to re-create without considerable cost. A 50/50 split agreement may seem steep, but it passive income. You as the landowner benefit by providing the land and the farm operator benefits by generating income without having to own any land whatsoever. It is a win-win situation for everyone involved. The farm operator will obviously have to own and operate their own equipment as well

MONEY GROWS ON TREES

as having to cover any costs related to the operation of the farm. At least they don't have to buy the land. If you currently own the land then you have to do not have make large capital expenses on things like tractors and paying wages. All that you do is buy the land. After you have bought the land, you can spend time finding farmers and farm operators that would be willing to work the land on a 50/50 basis with you. There are various crops that will produce high income for your farm including:

Grapes – There are many fruit juice manufacturers that would be interested in purchasing your grapes for the creation of their product. Grapes are a high yield crop that can generate substantial income for your farm.

MONEY GROWS ON TREES

Cotton – Your yield can be sold to be used as raw material for textile manufacturing.

Mushrooms – Mushroom farming can yield additional income for your farm and requires less space in contrast to grapes or cotton.

Sugarcane – Sugarcane is a high yield crop that will generate substantial income for your farm. It is used as sweetener in various products and is well sought after by drink manufacturers.

Tea – Tea is best grown in areas that experience heavy rainfall. Your crop can be sold to tea brands and sold wholesale.

MONEY GROWS ON TREES

Ginger – Ginger is a highly profitable crop that is used by candy manufacturers, drink manufacturers, and in supermarket aisles.

Rice – Rice is a high yield crop that can generate export sales for your farm.

Before Farming
You have to understand various factors that could affect your farm including:

Biotic – The ecosystem of the land including animals, insects, and pests affect your ability to produce.

Topography – The elevation, the slope, and the terrain will determine what you can grow.

MONEY GROWS ON TREES

Properties – PH, soil content, color, and texture will determine the health of your crop.

Viability – Are there enough buyers of a specific crop to justify its production? What is the demand chain model from your farm to the consumer?

Steps in Farming
Farming Model
Choosing Your Crop
Preparing Land
Sourcing Seeds
Planting Seeds
Irrigation of Crops
Biotic Growth Management
Harvesting

Farming Model – Are you going to farm the land or do a 50/50 split agreement

MONEY GROWS ON TREES

with a farming operator? Are you going to start a farming cooperative and share all the profits equally?

Choosing Your Crop – You obviously want to choose a crop that will be both high yield as well as being highly profitable.

Land Preparation – If the land needs to be irrigated or flattened in order to accommodate the growth of a specific crop, this must be done before planting seeds. Land has to be ploughed, leveled, and given manure in order to be ready for planting.

Sourcing Seeds – Certain seeds have to be sourced globally and require time to be fulfilled.

MONEY GROWS ON TREES

Planting Seeds – Seeds must be planted in a methodical and even fashion that allows for organized crop growth. Planting seeds, also known as sowing, can be done by hand or by machine.

Irrigation – Proper irrigation is important to achieving maximum crop growth.

Biotic Management – The area in which you are farming could be subject to wild animals, insects, pests, and pathogens that could affect your crop growth. It is important to have a plan to manage the various aspects of the ecosystem in which you are farming.

Harvesting – Harvesting is the gathering and picking of crop by hand or machine. Harvesting automation can reduce work injuries and increase productivity. In many cases, it is cheaper and faster to use humans for harvesting rather than make large capital expenditures on heavy machinery.

Urban Farming

For various reasons, it might become difficult for you to setup a traditional farm. Depending on your amount of space, you could set up an Urban Farm. An Urban Farm requires far less space is can be done in several locations. An Urban Farm can be setup on the rooftop of a building or it can be setup indoors inside a room. Urban Farming has the advantage of requiring less space, allowing you to save money on land expenditures and shifting those funds

MONEY GROWS ON TREES

towards equipment (lighting, watering). If you use the roof of a building, you are able to use natural sunlight and save money on lighting expenses all together. Urban Farmers use rooftops and indoor spaces for farming. In order to maximize space and to maximize the amount of plants and/or vegetables that are grown, multi-level free standing shelves are built. In the same space that a single row of tomatoes are grown, five other rows of tomatoes are vertically placed on top. Urban Farming requires ingenuity and adherence to total use of space in order to maximize crop production. Urban Farms have the advantage of being closer to consumer markets; Farmer's Markets, Grocery Chains, and other retailers, placing them at an advantage in comparison to traditional land farms. The notion that all

MONEY GROWS ON TREES

farming must be done on a farm is
wholly ludicrous as urban farms have
proven their ability to supply local
communities. Urban farming has gained
in steady popularity as major population
centers grew. Los Angeles, New York,
and other major cities feature urban
farming cooperatives supplying local
communities.

Farming Products

The Money Grows On Trees system
depends on creating multiple streams of
revenue. Your Farm can also generate
multiple streams of revenue from selling
raw fruits and vegetables to creating
finished products that can be sold in
stores. If you are growing strawberries
or tomatoes or oranges, for example,
you can turn these in to finished
products. Strawberries can be turned in

to fruit jam, syrup, or fruit juice. Tomatoes can be turned in to tomato paste or tomato juice. Oranges can be turned in to fruit juice. Farming products do not just have a wholesale value but also have value as a store bought finished product.

Logging

Approximately 100,000 Americans work in the logging industry. There are on average, 70 deaths per 100,000 workers in the logging industry. Health and Safety codes should be implemented before starting any logging operation. You can enter the logging industry as a landowner or as a logger. If you are starting out in the logging industry and you are not experienced with operating heavy machinery, it is better to start off as a landowner. As a timber landowner,

MONEY GROWS ON TREES

you can exploit the timber on your land by selling your timber to a logging company. A logging company will conduct a survey, known as a timber cruise, by surveying trees you have and paying you for the timber they will purchase. The value of your timber is referred to as your stumpage value. The stumpage value is determined by measuring the height and diameter of the trees and determining the volume. The stumpage value that you will be paid by the buyer is determined by your volume. Tree species differ vastly and will also help determine the final price you will be receiving. Some buyers choose to purchase by volume (cubic feet) and some choose to purchase by acre. For example, if you purchase 1 Acre of Land (43,560 Square Feet) for $2,000 in a wooded area, the Stumpage

MONEY GROWS ON TREES

Value of your land could be worth
$3,000 to $5,000 depending on the
thickness of your trees (10 inches or
more) and the height of your trees (9
feet tall or more). Trees with at least 10
inches in diameter and 9 feet tall or
more are referred to as saw timber and
are higher in quality in comparison to
pulpwood. In most situations, trees will
not be perfectly planted in rows with
perfect spacing between them. For
example, if you have 1 acre of land with
all the trees planted in rows with 20 feet
between rows of trees and 6 foot of
spacing between each tree, you would
be able to fit between 350 to 400 trees
on 1 acre of land. If you have 10 acres
of land, you could well have nearly 4000
trees. In most cases, there will be
several species of trees on your
property. Remember to get multiple

MONEY GROWS ON TREES

quotes from multiple buyers in order to maximize the amount of money you will ultimately receive. Let us say that you spent $100,000 purchasing 10 acres of heavily wooded land that contains 2,000 trees. If each tree sells on average for $200, then you just grossed $400,000. Your expenses are the $100,000 you spent to purchase the land. You just made a net profit of $300,000 before taxes and insurance. Your total capital outlay was the $100,000. You didn't have to cut a tree nor did you have to grow a tree. If you do choose to grow a tree and sell its lumber, it is better that you choose a tree to grow that has value. Below is a sample list of prices you can expect to receive when you are selling trees on your property.

MONEY GROWS ON TREES

10 Feet Tall and 12 Inches in Diameter Trees Sell Price Chart

(Approximations)

Fruit Wood $1,700

Mahogany $1,400

Rosewood $1,000

Teak $800

Black Walnut $350

White Oak $300

Cedar $300

Yellow Birch $300

Chestnut $300

Black Cherry $200

MONEY GROWS ON TREES

Eucalyptus $200

Red Oak $200

Maple $200

White Pine $150

Douglas Fir $100

Beech $100

Elm $100

Paper Birch $50

Poplar $30

There are many species of trees and
each has its own value. You should
always use multiple buyers in order to

MONEY GROWS ON TREES

get the highest price. If you use a Forestry Consultant, it is likely that you will be able to get a higher price from your trees but you will have to pay the Forestry Consultant a fee, usually 5 to 10 percent. The age of your wood will most certainly affect the price of your trees.

Age 0 – 5 Years Old Non-Durable

Age 5-10 Years Old Slightly Durable

Age 10-15 Years Old Moderately Durable

Age 15-25 Years Old Durable

25+ Very Durable

MONEY GROWS ON TREES

Defects in your trees can lower the price of your woodlot. Hardwoods such as maple and oak have higher values than softwoods like pine and fir.

The ultimate buyer is always the sawmill because they are going transform the wood in to workable raw materials that can be used for:

Construction

Furniture Building

Musical Instruments (Guitars, etc)

Sports Equipment

Kitchen Utensils

Housewares

Charcoal

MONEY GROWS ON TREES

Pallets

Paper

Tools

Wood is a highly valued commodity that has risen in value as the increase in demand for new homes continues to rise. The increase in demand in the past 10 years has been steep and it has become a seller's market with real estate owners being able to demand premium prices on their real estate. For the most part, building in the United States is tied to the timber industry and depends on being able to source timber at an affordable price so that the price of new homes will not be affected. The reality is that the price of new homes are affected every year because the price of

MONEY GROWS ON TREES

timber rises every year. Some years the price is relatively stable but during economic crises the price of timber has risen swiftly to keep up with inflation. Inflation is a reality that is unavoidable because the United States Government prints money to pay off debts and pay for other services. As new money is printed, new money enters the money supply and this directly causes inflation. The timber industry, like every other industry, is forced to raise its prices in order to hedge against the rising prices of goods and services. Wood is a commodity that is absolutely vital to construction of new homes and the rising of new home prices are both dependent on the rising price of timber as well as being dependent on various market conditions including inflation. Money Grows On Trees literally when

MONEY GROWS ON TREES

you invest in timber rich land. Before
buying timber land, you should have
completed an independent inspection as
to the value of the trees on the property.
This will allow you to make a better
decision before purchasing timber rich
land. Let us say for example that you
invest $100,000 in timber land and you
have $100,000 worth of timber on your
land. You pay $100,000 for the land and
you sell the timber for $100,000. The
land you own is now free. You can sell
the land for $50,000 and end up with a
profit of $50,000. Remember that you
paid $100,000 and you reaped
$150,000 from the land in little more
than a month. Not a bad profit for one
month. Timber is a valuable commodity
that will continue to rise in value as the
population of the earth increases and
resources become less available and

MONEY GROWS ON TREES

more expensive to extract. The Money Grows On Trees is not a Get Rich Quick scheme but rather a Grow Rich Slow scheme that depends on you spending years of your time gaining experience in doing real estate transactions involving timber as well as traditional real estate such as single family homes. Timber land is real estate just as a multi-family apartment complex is, but the difference is that with timber land, you can sell the timber and re-plant trees on your land that can also be sold at a later date. With timber land, you can sell the timber, sub-divide the land, and build single family homes on it (that you could rent out or sell in the future). With timber land, you could sell the trees on the land and then sell the mineral rights (gold mining claims, oil and gas claims) to your land. With timber land, you could

MONEY GROWS ON TREES

sell the trees on the land and then transform the land in to an agricultural farm. Timber land has many advantages that traditional real estate does not. Timber land is vital to sawmills and provides them with the necessary wood to create workable raw materials such as construction lumber.

Your Time

One of the secrets of making money is having information. Information drives your investments and information provides you with new and more viable opportunities. Reading the newspaper takes on a whole new meaning when you view it from the lens of a speculative investor. You are looking for indicators that could create changes in prices. A looming war in a 3rd world country could easily affect the prices of Gold and

MONEY GROWS ON TREES

Crude Oil. A deal like Brexit does send shockwaves through financial markets and cause certain commodities like Gold to rise. A new nation joining the Euro zone could cause the prices of the real estate in that nation to rise. When you look at a newspaper through the lens of a speculative investor, you begin to notice new things. You begin to notice events and you will start to ask yourself how these events affect financial markets. Reading news about an oil glut and oil dumping could give you clues as to the direction that oil prices will go towards. You have to keep abreast of the latest news in order to understand what events are occurring. Once you understand the events occurring, you can begin to try to speculate as to how the financial markets and certain commodities will behave. Whether you

MONEY GROWS ON TREES

are Bullish or Bearish regarding financial markets, you have to stay aware of the next event that will take place. Once you have analyzed the event and the players involved, you can begin to try to draw conclusions as to how the players in this event will act. Information is the lifeline of speculative investors. Without constant flow of information, speculative investors will be hard pressed to make a decision, if any. This is why companies pay thousands of dollars per year for software that feeds them information. This information allows them to stay informed as well as be able to make informed decisions regarding financial matters. Speculative investing is information driven and will continue to be as long as events affect financial markets. Some would argue that money "makes the world go around" but a truer

MONEY GROWS ON TREES

statement would be that "information makes the money that makes the world go around". Information is expensive and time consuming to gather. Consultants are hired by speculative investors specifically because they have the information already available. Consultants can tell you the price of Cocoa on an actual farm in the Ivory Coast while the news channels and news sources can only tell you the price of Cocoa on global financial markets. A professional paid consultant has spent years gathering information that they "rent" to speculative investors and companies. It would be too cost intensive and time intensive to gather this information yourself, but by hiring a professional consultant you can save the time and money you would have wasted trying to re-create what they

MONEY GROWS ON TREES

have already achieved. Information is part of the winning formula for a business and without a steady flow of it, there is difficulty in top level decision-making. Decision-making is based on available and new information. Consultants have amassed "best practices" that allow them to offer you information not available to the public. Inflation is an unfortunate reality. The price of everything, from houses to land to Gold, rise over time. Inflation is caused when the supply of money is increased by the Government in order to pay off debt. If you look at a chart of inflation over the past 100 years, you will notice a pattern. Inflation has been a constant reality over the past 100 years and will continue to be an issue as long as Governments print money to pay off their debt. A 5 bedroom house in Los

MONEY GROWS ON TREES

Angeles would have cost approximately $50,000 in the early 1970's. That same house is nearly $1,000,000. The price of Gold was $36 an ounce 50 years ago. How much is it today? As of this writing, it is nearly $2,000 an ounce. You can see that inflation results in the prices of commodities and goods rising because the cost of production and the cost of labor has increased over time to keep up with the rate of inflation. In order to keep up with inflation, you have to increase your income over time. The higher the rate of return the more assured you are that you will beat inflation over time. Some financial vehicles such as Gold or Real Estate have done well in beating inflation. Some financial vehicles such as Stocks have had mixed records (some wins and some losses) against inflation. Whatever

MONEY GROWS ON TREES

financial vehicle or vehicles you choose
to beat inflation, you must realize that
inflation is a constant variable that must
be taken in to consideration when
choosing which financial vehicle to
invest in. All financial vehicles are not
equal and some have a better ability to
fight off inflation. Inflationary techniques
used to boost economies such as
Quantitative Easing are controversial
because their effects are not always
visible. Inflation hurts economies
because it creates instability in markets.
Your time should be spent and invested
where you are able to see the highest
return. If buying and selling timber on
timber land works for you then do that. If
buying single family homes works for
you then do that. If buying multi-family
apartment complexes works for you,
then do that. The point is to create

MONEY GROWS ON TREES

multiple streams of revenue (hopefully passive). That is the point of the entire Money Grows On Trees system. Create multiple streams of revenue and allow them to help you grow and fund more ventures. It is ultimately your time, and you have to decide where to put it. If buying farm land and leasing it out on a 50/50 split agreement works for you, then do that. Do that which you believe will create multiple streams of passive income for you. There is no single way to achieve success rather it has been shown that millionaires have 7 or more income streams that fuels them.

MONEY GROWS ON TREES

Business Books (Paperback)

25 Principles of Strategy
amazon.com/dp/1942825129

Secrets of Making Money
amazon.com/dp/0991028597

Grow Rich
amazon.com/dp/1942825439

Money Grows On Trees

www.ingramcontent.com/pod-product-compliance
Lightning Source LLC
Chambersburg PA
CBHW072021060426
42449CB00033B/1394